DANDELIONS

EVE BUNTING

DANDELIONS

Illustrated by
GREG SHED

HARCOURT BRACE & COMPANY
Orlando Atlanta Austin Boston San Francisco Chicago Dallas New York
Toronto London

This edition is published by special arrangement with
Harcourt Brace & Company.

Dandelions by Eve Bunting, illustrated by Greg Shed. Text
copyright © 1995 by Eve Bunting; illustrations copyright
© 1995 by Greg Shed. Reprinted by permission of Harcourt
Brace & Company.
Printed in the United States of America

ISBN 0-15-307536-8

8 9 10 025 99

To the librarians and teachers of Nebraska,
with special thanks to James E. Potter, historian,
Nebraska State Historical Society,
for his help.
—E. B.

To Lila and Jim, my parents,
and to Sharon, my wife, whose love and support
made this possible. With thanks to Hoyt,
Katie, and Stephanie.
—G. S.

We came to Nebraska Territory in the spring.

Our oxen, Brownie and Blackie, pulled the wagon and our cow, Moo, was tied on behind.

It was a long way from my grandparents' home in Illinois. A long, long way.

Papa laughed and sang. "Look at it, Emma," he said to Mama. "Miles and miles of free land."

"But it's so lonely . . . ," Mama said.

"We won't be lonely," Papa promised. "We have each other and the girls, and in the fall there will be the new baby." His voice sounded almost holy. "A new baby in a new land."

My little sister, Rebecca, put her mouth close to my ear. "Where are the trees, Zoe?"

"We'll come to some," I said.

We did. But not many.

Day after day we trundled along, our wagon wheels making their own tracks through the tall grass.

"See how the grass closes behind us?" Mama asked. "It's as if we'd never been."

We cooked our meals outside the wagon and slept on Mama's quilts spread on the ground. Papa told us the names of the stars and about the moon, how it rose and set, and how the moon and the stars were the same ones that shone over Grandma and Grandpa's house. The very ones we used to see through our bedroom window.

When he told us that I cried a little, but I didn't let Rebecca see.

The sound of the wind in the grass was like the sound of the rivers we'd known back home. Day and night the sound was in our ears.

Sometimes we came to real rivers, and when we did we washed ourselves and topped up our water kegs. Sometimes a river was easy to cross and sometimes hard, with Brownie and Blackie so frightened as they swam, and us holding on to them and to the wagon, too. Sometimes we even had to cross on a ferry pulled by ropes.

It had been weeks since we started our journey. Twelve miles a day, if we were lucky. One day we did seventeen.

Then, on a morning when the roar of the grass seemed quieter,
Papa jumped down from the wagon and shouted, "We're here!"

It looked no different from any of the land we'd crossed already.

"How do you know this is ours?" I asked.

Papa showed me wooden signs with our name—Bolton—on them.
He pulled one from the ground and waved it around. "See? My claim
stake. I planted it here when I came last spring." He held the sign
high and raised his face to the sky. "We're here!" he called again.
I thought maybe this time he was talking to God.

I will never forget the way Mama looked as she got down from the wagon and stood in the knee-high grass. She shaded her eyes.

"This is where we are to live our lives?" she asked Papa and her voice was as still as the land around us. "There is no water."

Papa smiled. "I told you we'll have to sink a well. The water is below. All we need is a pick and a shovel and those we brought."

"Couldn't we live beside the river?" Rebecca asked. "I liked it by the river." Her lips quivered.

"All that land is taken, 'Becca. But we'll do fine here. You'll see."

He put a hand on Mama's shoulder. "After the well is sunk we'll put in the crops. It's almost past seeding time. And then we'll start on the house." He slipped his arm down so it circled her waist. "Those neighbors I visited? The Svensons? They are just a three-hour ride farther on. They will advise us, and I am going to borrow their plow. We will go there before we settle."

We started for the Svensons' the very next morning. It was hard to see their house; it was so much like the empty land around it. I think we would have missed it if Papa hadn't known exactly where he was going. I don't know how he did know, but Papa is smart.

Mrs. Svenson came running toward us, and Papa stopped the wagon so Mama could get down. She and Mrs. Svenson met and hugged and cried.

"Does Mama know her already?" I whispered to Papa.

"No. But they are happy to see each other. It has been a long time since either of them has seen another woman." He sounded sad, but Papa is never sad for long. "It will be different soon. Other settlers will come."

"The ones that will live by the river?" Rebecca asked.

"Those and others. It will be crowded. Already there is the town I told you about, only a day's ride from here. There will be many towns."

I looked around. It was hard to imagine.

"Come see our house," Mr. Svenson called.

It was made of sods, chunks like bricks cut from the ground, and it had one door and one window that Mr. Svenson had bought for $1.25 in town. He kept touching the window as if he couldn't believe it was there.

The house was called a soddie. In it was a chunk stove they'd brought with them from Minnesota, a bed, a table, and benches.

They also had five boys, and a pig that they kept in a pit and a canary they kept in a cage. 'Becca and I liked the pig and the canary.

The Svensons shared their dinner with us. Mama admired the beautiful tablecloth that was spread on the table. Her fingers traced the flowers. "Roses," she said. "Remember the way they smell?"

"I remember," Mrs. Svenson said.

Bits of earth kept falling from the roof as we ate and Mrs. Svenson kept picking them off the table. Twice black beetles fell, too. "You get used to it," she said.

"Once a snake this big dropped." One of the boys spread his arms wide and leered at Rebecca and me.

I guess we were supposed to faint.

We didn't.

The canary sang a little song, and we all turned to look at it.

"I missed the songbirds," Mrs. Svenson said. "There are so few here. Mr. Svenson got me the canary."

"Its song is sweet," Mama said. "So sweet." I think it was tears that made her eyes shine.

We stayed over that night, Mama and Papa sleeping on the floor inside the soddie, all of us children outside.

"Are you girls afraid of mice?" the middle boy asked. "There are millions of them. They run over you. They'll probably nest in your hair."

"Rebecca and I like mice," I told him.

We pointed out the stars and told the boys their names. Castor and Pollux and Leo the Lion to the east. But they laughed their horrible, hooting laughs and said we were making it up. Only people and animals had names, they said.

We left early next morning, the plow in the wagon, our water kegs refilled.

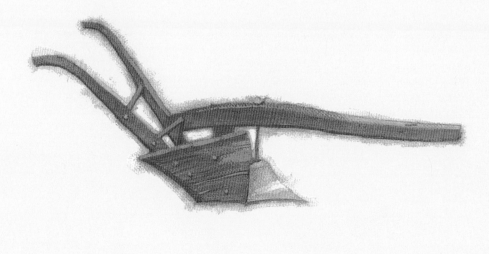

Mr. Svenson gave Papa a tree branch to use as a ridgepole for our house and two forked tree limbs from the river that would help hold the sod on our roof. He and Papa talked about how it would be done and Mr. Svenson said he'd come lend a hand. Papa said that he would be obliged. He said that he had three strong helpers of his own, too. He meant us, and he sounded so proud I felt we could do anything.

"Good neighbors," he told Mama as we rattled along. He and Rebecca and I walked beside the wagon because it was so heavy, with the plow and the wood and Mama and Mama's baby that was getting bigger inside of her.

"Will our house be just like theirs?" Mama asked.

Papa glanced at her sideways, then nodded. "I'll get us a window and a canary, too," he promised.

Papa said the first thing we must do was make slits in the ground and plant corn. That way we would have food for us and the animals for the coming winter. Then we started on the well. We dug a long way down. It was days before we found water.

"My gosh! We almost dug ourselves a hole into China," Papa boomed.

"To China? Truly?" Rebecca asked, and Papa laughed and drew up a bucket of cloudy water. He let the specks of dirt in it settle so we could all have a drink.

In the next weeks we cleared the land of hidden rocks and turned the earth and planted the rest of the seed we'd brought from home.

"Don't you see?" Papa asked Mama one night. I don't think he knew I was listening. "I could never have made a life for us in Illinois. It will be good here." It was as if he was pleading with her, and I felt sorry for him though I wasn't sure why.

When the house was up at last, Papa gave thanks for our snug soddie, for the baby that was to come, and for our safe journey. Mares-tail clouds waved in the sky and the grass sang around us. I'd never seen Papa so happy or Mama so sad.

I knew she missed our grandparents' house in Illinois where she'd lived all her life. Where we'd lived, too, until Papa decided to move west. That house had walls covered with pretty paper and a cupboard with painted china plates inside. Mama didn't say she was remembering that, but I knew.

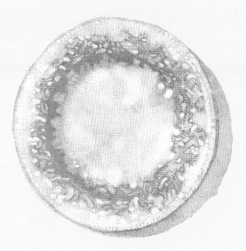

When we'd done our chores and finished our lessons, Rebecca and I always went to play outside.

"Don't get lost," Mama would whisper.

"We're only going to pet Moo," we'd tell her. "Or to pretend in our rock pile." We'd saved every rock from the field and the pile could be anything — our very own mountain or castle or fort.

Sometimes we'd see her watching us from inside the door and I'd think, Mama worries over nothing. It was true that the soddie did disappear almost as you stepped away from it, turning into just another hump in the ground.

"It's like a prairie dog's burrow," Mama said.

"I bet prairie dogs like their burrows," I told her and Papa smiled. "That's my Zoe girl!"

Mama would stand for hours looking at the curve where grass and sky met. "Always nothing," she'd say. "Always the sameness."

I was glad when she spoke, even to herself. It was her silences that scared me. Sometimes I felt she'd gone away and I couldn't find her.

It was late summer now and scorching hot from red sunrise to red sunset.

Our supplies were running low.

Mama had a birthday, and we used the last of the flour to make johnnycakes. They were the best I'd ever tasted.

One day Papa said, "Mama and I have talked things over. I must take the wagon into town and stock up. Zoe will come with me. Rebecca and Mama will come as far as the Svensons'. They can have a nice visit there till we get back."

"But I want to go to town, too!" Rebecca screamed. "It's not fair. I don't want to stay with those horrible Svenson boys." Rebecca doesn't scream often. But not going to town was something to scream about.

"You will come next time," Papa promised her. "It is too far and too hot for Mama to make the trip. Mrs. Svenson understands about babies being born, and Mama will be safe there. Zoe is older and can be a help to me. You must be a help to Mama."

There was no more to be said.

I was very excited, but I tried not to show it because it would make Rebecca feel worse.

It took a lot of preparation but at last we were on our way with Moo tied behind us so she could be milked at the Svensons' and so she wouldn't be lonely while we were gone.

Our neighbors were glad to see us again. They made a list of things they wanted us to bring back for them, and soon Papa and I were off, our water kegs refilled to the tip-top.

"Matthew? Are you sure you can find your way back?" Mama called, running heavily after the wagon. "Can you mark your trail?"

"With bread crumbs?" Papa asked, smiling. "Try not to worry, Emma. We will be fine."

He and I were both quiet, knowing she would worry anyway.

At last Papa said, "There is a little extra money. We will get something pretty for Mama to mark her birthday. You can help me choose."

He spoke some more after that, and to me it seemed he was, like Mama, talking to himself though I was there.

"The heat is bad. I pray Emma can stand it. When the baby comes it will ease things for her. But there'll be hard times, and oh, I pray to God I've done right by her."

I didn't dare look at him until I felt him straighten up.

He smiled across at me. "Ah well, we will help each other, my Zoe. And we will help her."

I promised myself I'd be good, I'd be the best girl in the world, I would never worry Mama.

Papa pointed. "There it is," he said.

The town was lifting itself as if by magic out of the distance, small to begin with, growing bigger the closer we got.

There was a long, muddy street with just one shop that sold soft goods and guns and cigars. There were two saloons and a livery stable and even a hotel with a real dining room that had Food Served painted on a sign in front. I kept saying, "Look, Papa. Look!"

Wagons and mule teams and horses and people filled the street. My ears rang with the noise of voices and the whinnying and braying of the animals. I bobbed up and down on the wagon bench.

Papa and I chose a bottle of scent in Judd's Store for Mama. It smelled like the lilac tree in Grandma's yard, and I hoped it would make her happy, not sadder. Papa bought Rebecca and me each a licorice stick. I wanted so badly to keep mine, but I ate it right away. Afterward I thought I should have saved it for Mama. It could have been a present from me. But it was too late.

We slept in the wagon that night under our friendly stars, and next morning I begged Papa to drive us along Front Street one last time. The town was already noisy even though it was barely dawn. I saw a man with a dancing monkey. The monkey had a red jacket with braid on it. I saw a dog with only three legs. There'd be so much to tell Mama and 'Becca when we got home.

Papa was just turning the wagon on the far edge of town when I saw something.

"Papa! Papa, stop!" I shouted.

He whoaed to Brownie and Blackie, and we sat for a few seconds, just looking. There, on a patch of sandy ground where the grass began, was a yellow mass of dandelions. "Dandelions!" I whispered. "How did they get here?"

"Likely they started from seed brought by chance on a wagon."

I put my hands against my face. "Dandelions for Mama."

Papa got the spade and helped me, and we took a lot, roots and all.

"Look!" I said. "We're bringing a whole dandelion family."

Papa smiled.

I was worried that the heat would kill them before we got home. But Papa used a little of our precious water to wet down some sacking and we wrapped the plants carefully and laid them in the wagon.

Now I was impatient to leave.

All the way to the Svensons' I kept leaning back to check on the dandelions. The sky was a burning blue and the grass seemed tinged with red fire. "It's so hot already," I moaned. "Oh, what if we lose them, Papa?"

"Dandelions are strong," Papa said. "They'll survive."

"Like us." I glanced across at him.

"Like us," he agreed.

It was late afternoon when we got to the Svensons'. Mama and Rebecca came running to meet us, and I thought Mama would never stop hugging us.

"You're back. You found us," she whispered.

"Of course," Papa said, and I smiled to myself. When we had her dandelions planted we'd be able to see our house from everywhere, our own bright patch of golden yellow. She'd never have to worry about us getting lost again.

I'd asked Papa not to tell her about my surprise, and he'd decided to keep the scent, too, till we got home.

Rebecca ate her licorice stick on the way. She thought Papa had bought it for her because she'd missed the trip to the town, and she wanted to share with me. But I told her I'd eaten mine and to eat hers and I'd watch and suffer.

Partway along I whispered the dandelion secret to her, and she clapped her hands. Oh, the licorice smell that wafted from her breath. It made my mouth water.

As soon as we got home we gave Mama her scent. She loved it. She dabbed some on Rebecca and me. I watched her carefully, but she didn't seem to be remembering the old lilac tree, and I was glad for Papa.

I'm sure I didn't sleep at all that night, still holding the dandelion secret, waiting for morning. Late, late I felt Papa step carefully over Rebecca and me, and I heard him carry the dandelions onto the roof. He'd promised he would. Nice Papa.

The sun wasn't even up when Rebecca and I crept from under our quilts. We had two of Mama's cherished spoons, and we scraped trenches in the hard sod of the roof and set the dandelions in. They drooped and that worried me, but when we gave them water from the bucket, they looked better.

Below us we could hear Mama and Papa getting out of their bed.

"There's an animal on the roof again," Mama said, and Rebecca put her hand over her mouth to stop her giggles.

Then we heard Mama ask, "Where have the girls gone?" and we scrambled down from the roof and called, "We're here. Come outside, Mama."

Rebecca was jumping up and down. "Surprise!" she yelled.

We held Mama's hands and led her a few steps from the soddie. I pointed to the roof. "Look! Happy birthday, Mama!"

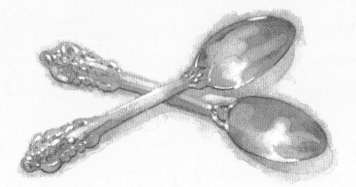

I'd wanted to see a golden blaze so dazzling it would hurt our eyes. But above us there was only a green stubble with a patch or two of wilted yellow.

"They're dandelions," I said, fighting down a rush of disappointment. "You can hardly tell."

"They're not very pretty, Zoe," Rebecca said. "I wish they were prettier."

"They will be," Papa said quickly. "They'll cover the roof and they'll shout: 'This is home!' But their roots have to take hold first, 'Becca. It isn't easy being transplanted."

"Maybe they'll never bloom," Mama said. "Maybe they'll just die of loneliness." Then she squeezed my hand. "Oh, Zoe! I'm sorry. I didn't mean . . . You were such a dear girl to think—"

I interrupted. "They'll bloom, Mama. They're strong, like us." I was almost crying and I didn't know why.

Mama and Papa were looking at each other. This was about more than the dandelions. I could feel it.

Then Mama gave a shaky little sigh.

The sun was rising, red on the line of distance as the four of us stood, looking at the roof. I hoped maybe one, just one, dandelion might lift its head for us. But not even one did.

Mama put her arm around my shoulder and pulled me close.

"Don't expect a miracle, Zoe. It will take time."

"Can you wait?" I asked, my voice muffled against her.

"I can wait," Mama said.